Ben *and the* Geocache Treasure

BY HEATHER GREGORY

TATE PUBLISHING *& Enterprises*

Published by Tate Publishing & Enterprises, LLC
127 E. Trade Center Terrace | Mustang, Oklahoma 73064 USA
1.888.361.9473 | www.tatepublishing.com

Tate Publishing is committed to excellence in the publishing industry. The company reflects
the philosophy established by the founders, based on Psalm 68:11,
"The Lord gave the word and great was the company of those who published it."

Book design copyright © 2011 by Tate Publishing, LLC. All rights reserved.
Cover and interior design by Elizabeth M. Hawkins
Illustrations by Jeff Elliott

Published in the United States of America

ISBN: 978-1-61346-135-8
Juvenile Nonfiction / Sports & Recreation / Games & Activities
11.05.16

For S and B,

my motivation and inspiration—causebe I did it!

"I'll get it!" Ben yelled as he watched the baseball roll to the edge of the hillside and down the embankment.

Ben trotted carefully down the slope to the edge of a thick, natural field. The ball had been moving pretty fast, and Ben could see it lying against the edge of a fallen tree about ten feet into a woodsy area. He walked carefully, lifting his legs over the tall grass, and approached the ball.

As Ben reached for the baseball, his eye caught a shine of blue from under a hollow place in the log. *What's that?* he thought.

He stepped closer to investigate the object. It was a small plastic box with a sticker that was smeared with mud and difficult to read. Ben squatted down to get a better look.

"Ben, let's go!" his dad shouted. "Time to head home!"

Ben quickly slipped the box inside his sweatshirt pouch. *Have to get this thing home before checking it out,* he thought.

In the car, Ben's head started whirling. *What could the box be? Who left it there? Why was it hidden?*

He had the find squirreled away out of his parents' view. *Sometimes a little secret from your folks is okay, isn't it?* he tried to convince himself.

As soon as his dad parked, Ben flew upstairs to his room and flopped onto the bed.

"Now," he whispered to the box, "let's see what we've got here."

Ben gently pried the plastic latch and heard a *pop!* He lifted the lid, revealing the contents. One by one, Ben removed the items and spread them on his blanket. He handled each quickly before moving on to the next: one plastic monkey, one rubber duck, a blue marble, a wooden disk with a South Carolina map, one baseball card, a pen, and a small notebook.

Ben was so occupied with inspecting the trinkets that he didn't hear the door open or notice his mom looking over his shoulder. "Whatcha got there, bud?" she asked.

Ben jumped and nearly fell off the bed in surprise.

"Uh," he answered nervously, "it's a box I found at the park. Honest, Mom, I found it hidden in a tree, like pirate treasure or something."

"Well," she said thoughtfully, "let's take a closer look at this treasure. We don't want any upset pirates stopping by."

She knelt down, and they examined the objects together. "Maybe there are clues in the notebook," Mom suggested.

Ben flipped the cover open and read a list of strange-sounding names. It looked like a secret code.

"I bet these are pirate names!" he said excitedly. "Listen to this, Mom. TDog, Dinky13, Wahoo. Don't these sound like pirate names?"

But Mom wasn't listening. "Look here," she said, pointing to the back of the notebook.

Mom read aloud, "Congratulations! You have just discovered a geocache. Remember to log your find. If you found it by accident, check out www.geocaching.com for more information on the exciting world of geocaching."

"What's a go-catch?" Ben asked.

"I'm not sure, buddy," Mom answered. "But we can find out."

She picked up the notebook, walked to Ben's computer, and helped him type a search for "geocaching." They began to read the results, but Ben stopped when he recognized two words: *treasure hunting*. "See, Mom?" he yelled. "Treasure! Gotta be pirates!"

Mom chuckled. "I think you might want to keep reading." 'Geocaching is a real-life treasure-hunting adventure. Searchers use a global positioning system (GPS) to find containers hidden around the world. Usually a container housing a logbook, pen, and treasure, geocaches are currently located in over a hundred countries and on all seven continents.'"

"Jee-o-cash," Ben pronounced slowly. "Hey, Mom, the note said to look at that website, right? Can we?"

★ = Easy

★ ★

★ ★ ★ = Medium

★ ★ ★ ★

★ ★ ★ ★ ★ = Hard

Ben and his mom read all afternoon. They learned about coordinates and people all over the world who hide and seek caches using GPSs. They discovered that geocachers respect nature, never burying the cache or disturbing the land. Often, geocachers hide trash bags inside the boxes so people can clean up the environment. Caches can be large, medium, or as small as a pencil eraser. One-star caches are easy to find, and five-star caches are a real challenge. They can be hidden in bushes, under rocks, or even under water.

Ben thought this was the coolest thing ever; real treasure hunting right there in his town! He could search for the rest of his life and never find every cache. There were over one million caches worldwide, and the number was growing every day.

But the more Ben read, the more something bothered him. He went back to look at the items lying on his bed. It was treasure, and he had found it. Finder's keepers, right? As he stared at the box, he imagined how frustrating it would be to search for something that wasn't there and how sad he would be if he were the one looking for the cache. Deep down he knew this wasn't his treasure. It belonged to the geocachers who would come looking for it. He had to return that box.

It took only a moment to replace the items and ask his parents to drive him back to the park. In the car, Ben held the cache gently in his lap. He felt even more excited than when he found the box. This time, he knew what he had and was part of the game. This time, he knew the secret of geocaching.

They reached the field, retraced the baseball's trail, and together located the fallen tree. Ben began to put the case back but then stopped to think. After a second, he turned, sat down on the log, and opened the box.

"I thought you were putting it back?" his Dad said.

"I am," Ben replied, "but I've got to do something first."

Ben removed the notebook and took out the pen. He turned to an empty page and wrote,

"Ben was here. I'm sory I tok the cache. I brot it back tho. Happy treshur huntin!"

With a smile, he closed the notebook and then placed the cache back into its true home.

"I'm proud of you, bud," his mom said as they climbed the hill.

"Me too," his dad added, scooping him up into a big bear hug.

"How proud?" Ben slyly asked between squeezes.

"Why?" his parents responded suspiciously.

"Well, I was thinking. Maybe we could get a GPS…"

Geo to Know

Cache: The container and treasure used in geocaching.

FTF: Means "First to find." The person who finds the cache before everyone else.

GPS: Global positioning system; a device that reads coordinates and gives directions.

Hitchhikers: Tags, bugs, or coins found in some caches. These unique items have registration numbers that allow geocachers to follow the item online as it moves between caches.

"Hucklebuckle!": A phrase yelled when the cache is sighted. This allows other hunters in the group to continue looking until everyone has found the cache.

Logbook: A notebook or paper located in the cache where finders record their identity and comments.

Muggles: Term (taken from the *Harry Potter* series) used to describe non-geocaching people.

SWAG: Treasure, usually small children's toys, found in the cache. Means "stuff we all get."

TFTC: An abbreviation commonly found in logbooks and online registration of finds, means "Thanks for the cache."

Waypoints: The coordinates of the cache, identified by longitude and latitude numbers. These are the numbers placed into the GPS unit to locate the geocache.

Happy Hunting!

e|LIVE

---

listen|imagine|view|experience

AUDIO BOOK DOWNLOAD INCLUDED WITH THIS BOOK!

In your hands you hold a complete digital entertainment package. In addition to the paper version, you receive a free download of the audio version of this book. Simply use the code listed below when visiting our website. Once downloaded to your computer, you can listen to the book through your computer's speakers, burn it to an audio CD or save the file to your portable music device (such as Apple's popular iPod) and listen on the go!

How to get your free audio book digital download:

1. Visit www.tatepublishing.com and click on the e|LIVE logo on the home page.
2. Enter the following coupon code:
   57b9-4ee8-dbf5-8833-2b82-310d-f911-a978
3. Download the audio book from your e|LIVE digital locker and begin enjoying your new digital entertainment package today!